TO THE
ELECT
OF
GOD

*A message to the followers
of Jesus Christ*

RON VETTER

authorHOUSE®

AuthorHouse™
1663 Liberty Drive
Bloomington, IN 47403
www.authorhouse.com
Phone: 1-800-839-8640

Published by AuthorHouse   02/22/2012

ISBN: 978-1-4685-5750-3 (sc)
ISBN: 978-1-4685-5749-7 (e)

Library of Congress Control Number: 2012903472

CONTENTS

PART D
The Blessed Life

Part E
Doctrines of Christianity

INTRODUCTION

Beginning with this foundational principle that we together hold to be true, which is, Jesus of Nazareth is indeed the Christ, the Son of God, and the Savior of the world. If you also believe this fundamental truth, let us then move together toward a more complete examination of our common salvation.

Brothers and sisters, this book exists so that you will not be led astray. While the message of this book was being revealed to me, I felt there had been a continual urge to write it down, so that the Holy Spirit might open your eyes and so that you could see these truths. Not that I am worthy, but because of my obedience to the faith, by the word of God, and by His abundant mercy and grace, God has chosen me for this work. You will notice that the word of God is quoted often throughout this book. The main goal was to present God's message in a clear way in hopes that you will understand His truth. Let Christ reveal to you whether or not this is His truth. For we should not ourselves be teachers of God's word; rather, we should direct people to what Jesus taught. Jesus is the teacher:

> *And don't let anyone call you 'Teacher,' for you have only one teacher, the Christ. (Matthew 23:10 NLT)*

The true teacher of Christ will direct others to what Jesus says:

> *Therefore go and make disciples of all nations, baptizing them in the name of the Father and of the Son and of the Holy Spirit, and teaching them to obey everything I have commanded you. (Matthew 28:19-20 NIV)*

The main idea here is to keep an open mind, for this is the key to understanding God's word. While writing this material, I experienced many revelations about God's word. For me, this was a fulfillment of God's word:

> *So pay attention to how you hear. To those who listen to my teaching, more understanding will be given. But for those who are not listening, even what they think they understand will be taken away from them. (Luke 8:18 NLT)*

Jesus warns us to take heed how we interpret the word of God. Jesus says that if you hear, more will be given. Therefore, work out your relationship with God so that you may hear from God for yourself. Then, let Jesus reveal the deep mysteries of His word, so that His light will shine in you and your light will light up a small part of this dark world. Our light together can shine so the world will be able to see what God really wants from His people, which is for His righteousness to shine through us. Truly everything that is good in this world is from God:

> *So don't be misled, my dear brothers and sisters. Whatever is good and perfect comes down to us from God our Father, who created all the lights in the heavens. He never changes or casts a shifting shadow. (James 1:16-17 NLT)*

It is also appropriate to talk about knowledge in general. The Bible tells us the beginning of all knowledge is fear of the Lord:

> *The fear of the Lord is the beginning of knowledge, but fools despise wisdom and discipline. (Proverbs 1:7 KJV)*

The fear of the Lord is to understand that God hates evil and administers justice accordingly.

> *Come, you children, listen to me: I will teach you the fear of the LORD. What man is he that desires life, and loves many days, that he may see good things? Keep your tongue from evil, and your lips from speaking guile. Depart from evil, and do good; seek peace, and pursue it. The eyes of the LORD are on the righteous, and his ears are open to their cry. The face of the LORD is against them that do evil, to cut off the remembrance of them from the earth. (Psalm 34:11-16 KJV)*

There is a lot in this book about how to get to heaven. Some might become discouraged that they will not be able to attain the kingdom of heaven. I would like to point out a scripture to the reader that suggests there is a judgment for all individuals, whether they are the elect or not. This judgment comes at the end of time and is dependent upon how we have treated our fellow mankind.

> *When the Son of Man comes in his glory, and all the angels with him, he will sit on his throne in heavenly glory. All the nations will be gathered before him, and he will separate the people one from another as a shepherd separates the sheep from the goats. He will put the sheep on his right and the goats on his left.*

Then the King will say to those on his right, 'Come, you who are blessed by my Father; take your inheritance, the kingdom prepared for you since the creation of the world. For I was hungry and you gave me something to eat, I was thirsty and you gave me something to drink, I was a stranger and you invited me in, I needed clothes and you clothed me, I was sick and you looked after me, I was in prison and you came to visit me.'

Then the righteous will answer him, 'Lord, when did we see you hungry and feed you, or thirsty and give you something to drink? When did we see you a stranger and invite you in, or needing clothes and clothe you? When did we see you sick or in prison and go to visit you?' The King will reply, 'I tell you the truth, whatever you did for one of the least of these brothers of mine, you did for me.'

Then he will say to those on his left, 'Depart from me, you who are cursed, into the eternal fire prepared for the devil and his angels. For I was hungry and you gave me nothing to eat, I was thirsty and you gave me nothing to drink, I was a stranger and you did not invite me in, I needed clothes and you did not clothe me, I was sick and in prison and you did not look after me.'

They also will answer, 'Lord, when did we see you hungry or thirsty or a stranger or needing clothes or sick or in prison, and did not help you?' He will reply, 'I tell you the truth, whatever you did not do for one of the least of these, you did not do for me.'

Then they will go away to eternal punishment, but the righteous to eternal life. (Matthew 25:31-46 NIV)

OUR CALLING

*At night my soul longs for You, Indeed, my spirit within me seeks You diligently; **For when the earth experiences Your judgments. The inhabitants of the world learn righteousness.** (Isaiah 26:9 NAS)*

The earth has experienced God's judgments. Jesus says:

Now is the judgment of this world: now shall the prince of this world be cast out. (John 12:31 KJV)

The time has come that the world should learn righteousness. Jesus said that we would be judged according to the word He spoke.

The one who rejects me and does not receive my words has something to judge him: The word that I have spoken will judge him on the last day. (John 12:48 ESV)

Moses also spoke of a judgment on anyone who would not hear Jesus's words. Moses confirms that these were actually God's word spoken to us.

I will raise them up a Prophet from among their brothers, like to you, and will put my words in his mouth; and he shall speak to them all that I shall command him. And it shall come to pass, that whoever will not listen to my words which he shall speak in my name, I will require it of him. (Deuteronomy 18:18-19 KJV)

Jesus also confirms that the words He spoke were God's words not His own.

For the words which You gave Me I have given to them; and they received them and truly understood that I came forth from You, and they believed that You sent Me. (John 17:8 NASB)

Therefore, our calling as Christians is to obey the word of God, and in doing so, we will become righteous not only in word, but also in deed. Being instructed in the way of righteousness, we will be able to teach others. This does not mean that we will not fail, for surely we will, but still we must strive. Elect of God, you are chosen by God if you overcome sin by having faith in Jesus, and by having the Spirit of Christ and by the grace of God, that you,

Having the eyes of your hearts enlightened, that you may know what is the hope of his calling, and what are the riches of the glory of His inheritance in the saints. (Ephesians 1:18 ASV)

Brothers and sisters, regardless of what some may say, do not let this truth escape your perception.

God will render to every man according to his deeds: To them who by patient continuance in doing good seek for glory and honor and

*immortality, eternal life: But to them that are contentious, and
do not obey the truth, but obey unrighteousness, indignation and
wrath, Tribulation and anguish, on every soul of man that does evil,
of the Jew first, and also of the Gentile. (Romans 2:6-9 NASB)*

Brothers and sisters, do not be deceived; Christ died on the cross so
that we might become righteous. If you reject this, you reject God.

*For God did not call us to uncleanness, but in holiness. Therefore
he who rejects this does not reject man, but God, who has also given
us His Holy Spirit. (1 Thessalonians 4:7-8 KJV)*

The Lord Jesus Christ himself has warned us that we must attain to
righteousness.

*For I tell you that unless your righteousness exceeds that of the scribes
and Pharisees, there is no way you will enter into the Kingdom of
Heaven. (Matthew 5:20 KJV)*

What we must understand is that if Jesus is our Lord, then we have to
obey him.

*Why do you call me, Lord, Lord, and do not do the things which I
say? (Luke 6:46 KJV)*

We have to be careful what we believe. We don't want to end up being
like the people spoken of here:

*These people honor me with their lips, but their hearts are far from
me. They worship me in vain; their teachings are but rules taught*

by men. You have let go of the commands of God and are holding on to the traditions of men. (Mark 7: 6-8 NIV)

God was in Christ, clarifying the commandments for us to follow. Incorrect teaching will make God's word of no effect. If the word is not understood, its hearers won't find the power of God.

Thus making void the word of God by your tradition that you have handed down. And many such things you do. (Mark 7:13 ESV)

The power of God is what we need in order to get to heaven, because we need His power in order to do His will. To inherit the kingdom of heaven, we have to do what God wants us to do. Jesus puts it this way:

Not everyone who says to me, Lord, Lord, will go into the kingdom of heaven; but he who does the will of my Father in heaven. (Matthew 7:21 KJV)

If heaven is our goal, then our calling is to do the will of God. God is seeking true worship. True faith should create people who behave like Christ. If we say we believe, yet don't do anything Christ tells us to do, how can we really believe we will be saved and go to heaven? Let us examine in more detail the true gospel of Jesus Christ. Let us give glory to God and to the Lord Jesus Christ for what they have done for us. Faith in Jesus and in the word of God has the power to transform our lives, but we must obey the word of God.

Jesus said to the people who believed in him:

You are truly my disciples if you remain faithful to my teachings.
(John 8:31 NLT)

Our calling as the children of God is to be righteous, for we should present ourselves as servants to Christ for the glory of God. May God give us the power to do it, Amen.

PART A

What Is Salvation?

*And she will bring forth a Son, and you shall call his name Jesus, for He will **save His people from their sins**. (Matthew 1:21 KJV)*

WHAT IS SALVATION?

This is a key question when it comes to our faith. As much as possible, we should try not focus on what other people say about our faith. Rather, we should focus on what the word of God says about our faith, because the word of God is the ultimate authority, not only in matters of life, but especially in matters that pertain to our faith. As Christians, we are blessed to have the complete word of God in the New and Old Testaments. In our examination of the deep topic of our salvation, we will look at both, because:

> *All scripture is given by inspiration of God, and is profitable for doctrine, for reproof, for correction, for instruction in righteousness. (2 Timothy 3:16 KJV)*

Let's begin our look at salvation with Jesus's name. Jesus is the Greek translation for the Hebrew name 'Joshua,' which means 'God the savior.' Jesus became an instrument with the sole purpose of fulfilling the will of God, that is, to save the world. As Christians, we have to continue God's work by spreading the truth about what the cross of Christ really means.

> *God was in Christ reconciling the world to Himself. (2 Corinthians 5:19 KJV)*

Jesus's name helps us define Salvation. Salvation is being saved from our sin. We know this is true because the word says so:

> *And she will bring forth a Son, and you shall call his name Jesus, for He will save His people from their sins. (Matthew 1:21 KJV)*

The word of God tells us that Jesus will save His people from their sins. Who, then, are His people? Let's let the word answer that:

> *For this reason I was born, and for this I came into the world, to testify to the truth. Everyone who is of the truth listens to me. (John 18:37 NIV)*

Therefore, God's people are those who hear the truth.

> *Jesus answered, "I am the way and the truth and the life. No one comes to the Father except through me. (John 14:6 KJV)*

Jesus warned us to take heed of how we interpret the word of God. In other words, we must be careful how we discern truth:

> *So pay attention to how you hear. To those who listen to my teaching, more understanding will be given. But for those who are not listening, even what they think they understand will be taken away from them. (Luke 8:18 NLT)*

It is worth repeating: *'Salvation' is being saved from our sins.* What does it mean to be saved from our sin? We are saved by the forgiveness of our sin, through the redemption that is in Christ. We are also saved from our sin by having the Spirit of Jesus Christ living in us. These two parts together make up our salvation. We must beware of people who try to tell us that salvation is anything else. Even if they have good intentions, they could lead us astray. Let God reveal what salvation is to you through the Word of God.

> *But now having been set free from sin, and having become slaves of God, you have your fruit to holiness, and the end, everlasting life. For the wages of sin is death, but the gift of God is eternal life in Christ Jesus our Lord. (Romans 6: 22-23 KJV)*

Do not be misled; God's gift is being set free from sin, and the result is eternal life. If we continue in sin, then death and judgment will be the result. We have to understand that God decides who will be saved and who will not be saved.

> *Then Jesus said to them again, "I am going away and you will seek Me, and you will die in your sin. Where I go you cannot come. (John 8: 21 KJV)*

Some people want us to believe that salvation is being set free from the penalty of sin, without being set free from sin itself. Being freed from the penalty of sin is the result of being freed from sin.

> *And you shall know the truth, and the truth shall set you free. (John 8:32 KJV)*

The truth shall set you free from committing sin! Do not listen to man, but listen to what the word of God says.

Whoever has been born of God does not sin, for His seed remains in him; and he cannot sin, because he has been born of God. (1 John 3:9 KJV)

People will say, "So you don't sin?" The truth is that everyone sins. However, the idea here is that God has provided the way for us to overcome sin, and we need to strive for this. Salvation is working together with God to remove sin from our lives. For this is the will of God: our sanctification.

For this is the will of God: your sanctification. (1 Thessalonians 4:3 KJV)

Perfection is the goal, and God is the judge. This is the power of the cross. This is the power of the gospel of Jesus Christ.

For I am not ashamed of the gospel of Christ, for it is the power of God to Salvation for everyone who believes. (Romans.1:16 KJV)

Salvation is a journey we take with God, with the ultimate goal of being like our master, Jesus Christ.

Him we preach, warning every man and teaching every man in all wisdom, that we may present every man perfect in Christ Jesus. (Colossians 1:28 KJV)

The scripture above says we are warned and taught so that we may become perfect. In the end, God will be the judge and will judge each one of us according to what we have done. Take heed that you don't reject this salvation that Christ went to the cross for, a salvation that has the power to make us become the righteous people God wants us to be.

SALVATION IN A MOMENT IN TIME

There are a lot of Christians who talk about the moment in the past when they were saved. The problem with this idea is that salvation is not something that happens at a moment in time. Our salvation continues on for as long as we do. If someone has convinced you that you are saved, you should seriously reconsider that idea. If you are convinced that you are saved, then you have discontinued God's work in your life because you think your salvation is complete. God is the judge of whether we are saved or not. Being saved means we are no longer serving sin, but that we are serving God. We need to ask ourselves this question every day. We have to live out our salvation every day.

> *Therefore, my dear friends, as you have always obeyed—not only in my presence, but now much more in my absence—continue to work out your salvation with fear and trembling. (Philippians 2:12 NIV)*

Notice Paul says to *continue* to work out your salvation. Paul did not want believers to just accept, without any questions, their salvation as complete. We can see this very clearly in the following scripture by Paul:

Examine yourselves as to whether you are in the faith. Prove yourselves. Do you not know yourselves, that Christ is in you?—unless indeed you are disqualified. (2 Corinthians 13:5 KJV)

We should not think that salvation can be acquired so easily when salvation was something for which the prophets had to search diligently.

Concerning this salvation the prophets sought and searched diligently, who prophesied of the grace that should come unto you. (1 Peter 1:10 KJV)

We know that the Prophets came before Christ. They also foresaw that some people still would not find the righteousness God was offering, in spite of His grace.

Let grace be shown to the wicked, yet he will not learn righteousness. (Isaiah 26:10 KJV)

With the grace and forgiveness He offers us through the cross, God clears us from our debt of sin. In our new relationship with God, we should become righteous by being obedient to His word. We also will receive the Spirit of God to help us overcome sin. These three parts together make up our salvation. If you reject this truth, then you have not truly considered why Jesus went to the cross, and you have rejected His message.

For God did not call us to uncleanness, but in holiness. Therefore he who rejects this does not reject man, but God, who has also given us His Holy Spirit. (1 Thessalonians 4:7-8 KJV)

"Salvation" without the ability to stop sinning is not salvation at all.

> *Strive to enter in by the narrow door, for many, I tell you, will seek*
> *to enter in, and will not be able. (Luke 13:24)*

Paul is credited for doing more for Christ than anyone. Yet, here we have Paul: beaten, jailed, stoned, and much more, time and time again. Still Paul says he has not achieved his goal, and presses on. How can we think that we will receive salvation so easily?

> *Not as though I had already attained, either were already perfect:*
> *but I follow after, if that I may apprehend that for which also I am*
> *apprehended of Christ Jesus. Brothers, I count not myself to have*
> *apprehended: but this one thing I do, forgetting those things which*
> *are behind, and reaching forth to those things which are before, I*
> *press toward the mark for the prize of the high calling of God in*
> *Christ Jesus. (Philippians 3:12-14 KJV)*

Some will say, "The scripture says,"

> *For by grace are you saved through faith; and that not of yourselves:*
> *it is the gift of God. (Ephesians 2:8 KJV)*

But I say to you, continue to read on.

> *For we are His workmanship, created in Christ Jesus for good*
> *works, which God has before ordained that we should walk in*
> *them. (Ephesians 2:10 ESV)*

As a new creation in Christ, are you being created by God? We have to walk in what God has prepared for us so that we can enter the Kingdom of Heaven. If we examine the context of Ephesians chapter two, we see that in this context, "saved" means we are no longer living in sin, and have been *saved* from walking as the rest of the world walks.

> *And you were dead in the trespasses and sins in which you once walked, following the course of this world, following the prince of the power of the air, the Spirit that is now at work in the sons of disobedience—among whom we all once lived in the passions of our flesh, carrying out the desires of the body and the mind, and were by nature children of wrath, like the rest of mankind. (Ephesians 2:1-3 ESV)*

We have to walk in that which God has prepared for us, then we can have hope that we will enter the kingdom of God.

THE HOPE OF SALVATION

Elect of God, do not be deceived. The Bible clearly tells us that salvation is to be hoped for, not taken as a sure thing. See here all these testimonies, not of man, but of the Word of God. Is your heart open?

> *Having the eyes of your hearts enlightened, that you may know what is the hope of his calling, and what are the riches of the glory of his inheritance in the saints. (Ephesians 1:18 ESV)*

Believe the Word of God. Hope leaves us seeking for that which we do not have.

> *For in this hope we were saved. But hope that is seen is no hope at all. Who hopes for what he already has? But if we hope for what we do not yet have, we wait for it patiently. (Romans 8:24-25 NIV)*

God is seeking followers who continually seek him and wait on him.

> *For we, through the Spirit, by faith wait for the hope of righteousness. (Galatians 5:5 KJV)*

We can continually improve our relationship with God if we have hope for our salvation.

> *Sanctify the Lord God in your hearts; and always be ready to give an answer to everyone who asks you a reason concerning the hope that is in you, with humility and fear. (1 Peter 3:15 KJV)*

By having hope for our salvation instead of thinking our salvation is complete, our faith will:

> *Present you holy and blameless and unreproveable in his sight: If you continue in the faith grounded and settled, and be not moved away from the hope of the gospel, which you have heard. (Colossians 1:23 KJV)*

This hope will be a fulfillment of the word for us.

> *To those who go on with good works in the hope of glory and honor and salvation from death, he will give eternal life. (Romans 2:7 KJV)*

We must continue with our good works. Although it will not always come with ease:

> *Now I stand here to be judged for the hope of the promise made by God to our fathers, which our twelve tribes, earnestly serving night and day, hope to attain. Concerning this hope I am accused by the Jews, King Agrippa! (Acts 26:6-7 KJV)*

As the word of God says, we must have hope of the promise and not merely believe that we have already received it. You see, if we have hope for something, then we are looking for it. We are working to make it happen and we are seeking it out. On the other hand, if we believe we have already received something when in fact we have not, then we will never find it. Jesus also confirms this idea of being locked out or blinded by saying, "I know the answer."

> *Jesus said to them, If you were blind, you should have no sin: but now you say, we see; therefore your sin remains. (John 9:41 NIV)*

We must be careful when we say, "I see."

LIVING WITHOUT SIN

Whoever says that perfection is unattainable is a liar. It is our responsibility to speak the truth. According to the word of God, perfection is attainable.

> *Therefore you shall be perfect, just as your Father in heaven is perfect. (Matthew 5:48 WEB)*

Jesus says if you behave in the manner described in chapters five, six and seven of the gospel of Matthew, you shall be perfect. This is not about boasting about how righteous we can become; it is about behaving the way God wants us to and knowing the truth. We have to be open to the idea that perfection is attainable through the forgiveness the cross of Christ gives us, by having the Spirit of God working in us, and being obedient to the word of God. It's about knowing that we are required by God to live righteously.

> *For the Grace of God that brings Salvation has appeared to all men, teaching us that, denying ungodliness and worldly lust, we should live soberly, righteously, and godly in the present age. (Titus 2:11-12 KJV)*

This idea is very important. Let's take a close look at some more scriptures to understand this truth. We should never make the claim that we are totally without sin; we are improving, continually working on getting sin out of our lives.

> *Whoever is born of God does not commit sin; for his seed remains in him: and he cannot sin, because he is born of God. In this the children of God are manifest, and the children of the devil: whoever does not practice righteousness is not of God, neither is he that does not love his brother. (1 John 3:9-10 KJV)*

This doesn't mean that we are without sin. It means that salvation is a process of allowing God to remove sin from our lives.

> *If we say that we have no sin, we deceive ourselves, and the truth is not in us. If we confess our sins, he is faithful and just to forgive us our sins, and to cleanse us from all unrighteousness. (1 John 1:8-9 KJV)*

Through Christ, God will cleanse us from all our sin, because He loves us and this is the best thing for us. This is the relationship we must have with God in order to be saved: one in which God is removing sin from our life. We see this relationship here in the book of John:

> *I am the true vine, and my Father is the farmer. Every branch in me that doesn't bear fruit, he takes away. Every branch that bears fruit, he prunes, that it may bear more fruit. You are already pruned clean because of the word which I have spoken to you. Remain in me, and I in you. As the branch can't bear fruit by itself,*

unless it remains in the vine, so neither can you, unless you remain
in me. (John 15:1-4 WEB)

Christ died on the cross so we could become righteous. His life, death, and resurrection are our salvation if we have his word and Spirit in us. We must be like Christ and pray for His Spirit to help us be righteous. It is by the resurrection that we are made perfect. Paul comments on this several times.

> *But if the Spirit of him that raised up Jesus from the dead*
> *dwell in you, he that raised up Christ from the dead shall also*
> *quicken your mortal bodies by his Spirit that dwells in you.*
> *(Romans 8:11 KJV)*

Reconciliation starts when we accept and confess Jesus is the Savior. Our salvation is accomplished by His resurrected Spirit living in us and by Him making intercession for us, as we see in the scripture below. Christ makes intersession with God for us. His Spirit lives in us and gives us power to become righteous.

> *For since our relationship with God was restored by the death of*
> *his Son while we were still his enemies, we will certainly be saved*
> *through the life of his Son. (Romans 5:10 KJV)*

Paul says that we must die, like Christ died, so we can be resurrected as Christ was resurrected.

> *What shall we say then? Shall we continue in sin, that grace may*
> *abound? May it never be! We who died to sin, how could we live*
> *in it any longer? Or don't you know that all we who were baptized*

into Christ Jesus were baptized into his death? We were buried therefore with him through baptism to death, which just like Christ was raised from the dead through the glory of the Father, so we also might walk in newness of life. (Romans 6:1-4 WEB)

To walk in newness of life, with the Spirit of God living in us—this is being born again. This is living without sin. God did not make Jesus become sin and die on the cross to pardon us from all of our sin. As the scripture says, Jesus died on the cross *so that we might **become** the righteousness of God.*

God was in Christ reconciling the world to himself, not imputing their trespasses to them; and has committed to us the word of reconciliation. Now then we as ambassadors for Christ, as though God were pleading through us: we implore you on Christ's behalf, be reconciled to God. For he has made Him who knew no sin to be sin for us, that we might become the righteousness of God in him. (2 Corinthians 5:19-21)

Through God's forgiveness in Christ and by His Spirit, *we are being saved from our sin,* because now we have a relationship with God through Christ, not by our works, but by His grace and obedience to the word of God. God reveals Himself in us when we believe and surrender to him.

Blessed are they which do hunger and thirst after righteousness: for they shall be filled. (Matthew 5:6 KJV)

To further illustrate this point, let's ask ourselves a question. Did Jesus teach us not to sin?

So if your hand or your foot causes you to sin, cut it off and throw
it away. It is better for you to enter life injured or crippled than
to have two hands or two feet and be thrown into eternal fire.
(Matthew 18:8)

Jesus is not telling us that we should cut our hands off, but how important it is that we should not sin. It is more important than our very limbs, because if we live in sin, we can't go to heaven.

Jesus said therefore again to them, "I am going away, and you will
seek me, and you will die in your sins. Where I go, you can't come.
(John 8:21 WEB)

PART B

How Are We saved?

Brothers, what shall we do?" And Peter said to them, "Repent and be baptized every one of you in the name of Jesus Christ for the forgiveness of your sins, and you will receive the gift of the Holy Spirit. (Acts 2:37-38 ESV)

HOW ARE WE SAVED?

So then, what must we do to attain our salvation? Here is what Peter answered when asked that same question:

> *And they said to Peter and the other apostles, "Brothers, what shall we do?" Peter replied, "Repent and be baptized, every one of you, in the name of Jesus Christ for the forgiveness of your sins. And you will receive the gift of the Holy Spirit. The promise is for you and your children and for all who are far off—for all whom the Lord our God will call. (Acts 2:36-39 ESV)*

To repent means to have regret for your sin and to turn from it. Baptism should be conducted by a pastor, a priest, or someone filled with the Spirit. Baptism washes away our sin.

> *And now why tarry? Arise, and be baptized, and wash away your sins, calling on the name of the Lord. (Acts 22:16 KJV)*

Another explanation is that baptism is a means of forgiveness for our sin.

> *Peter replied, "Each of you must repent of your sins and turn to God, and be baptized in the name of Jesus Christ for the forgiveness*

of your sins. Then you will receive the gift of the Holy Spirit. (Acts 2:38 NLT)

Baptism is a requirement of salvation because it is a fulfillment of righteousness. When Jesus went and was baptized by John the Baptist, John said to Jesus, I have a need to be baptized by you.

> *Jesus answered him "Let it be so now, for thus it is fitting for us to fulfill all righteousness." Then he consented. (Matthew 3:15 ESV)*

Notice that Peter says if you repent and are baptized, you will receive the gift of the Holy Spirit. This is the process we should follow to receive our salvation. Once we repent and are baptized, we have to wait for God to endow us with the Holy Spirit.

> *As soon as they arrived, they prayed for these new believers to receive the Holy Spirit. The Holy Spirit had not yet come upon any of them, for they had only been baptized in the name of the Lord Jesus. Then Peter and John laid their hands upon these believers, and they received the Holy Spirit. (Acts 8:16 NLT)*

When we receive the Spirit, we are born again. There are different ways to receive the Holy Spirit; however, this is an act of God and can only be accomplished by God.

BECOMING BORN AGAIN

Being born again is being born of the Spirit of God. This means that God and Christ live inside of us.

> *Do you not know yourselves, that Christ is in you?—unless indeed*
> *you are disqualified. (2 Corinthians 13:5 KJV)*

When we repent and are baptized, this is the beginning of the process of becoming born again. We should make an attempt to turn from sin and follow God's word. When God is ready, He will indwell us with the Holy Spirit, and we will become born again of the Spirit of God. Being born again means God has given us the opportunity to become the children of God. We see this spoken of in John:

> *But as many as received Him, to them He gave them the right to*
> *become children of God, to those who believe on his name: who*
> *were born, not of blood nor of the will of the flesh nor of the will of*
> *man, but of God. (John 1:12-13)*

Notice the wording; He gave them the *right to become*. After we are born again, we still have to become the children of God. We go through a process of growing up in our spiritual life. When we become born again, in spiritual terms we are only babies. Paul spoke of the idea of being an infant in the Lord:

> *And I, brothers, could not speak to you as to spiritual, but as to carnal, even as to babes in Christ. I have fed you with milk, and not with meat: for till now you were not able to bear it, neither yet now are you able. (1 Corinthians 3:1-2 KJV)*

As we study the word, follow the teachings of Christ, and receive the Spirit of God, we grow into spiritual adulthood, the goal being to become like Christ and completely obedient to Jesus's teachings. This is not easy; it takes continual striving to obey Jesus's teachings because they are divine wisdom. We have to be careful, for regardless of what some may say, we can lose our salvation. Listen to Jesus:

> *But the ones on the rock are those, when they hear, receive the word with joy; and these have no roots, who believe for a while, and in time of temptation fall away. (Luke 8:13 KJV)*

Peter says that not only can you can lose your salvation, but also you will be worse off if you fall away:

> *For if after they have escaped the pollutions of the world through the knowledge of the Lord and Savior Jesus Christ, they are again entangled therein, and overcome, the latter end is worse with them than the beginning. (2 Peter 2:20 KJV)*

As Peter says in the scripture above, if you are truly saved and then get entangled in and overcome by sin, then you have lost your salvation.

What does it mean to be truly saved? It means we are no longer living in sin.

> *In which you used to live when you followed the ways of this world*
> *and of the ruler of the kingdom of the air, the spirit who is now at*
> *work in those who are disobedient. (Ephesians 2:2 NIV)*

This is why salvation is something we strive for. As Jesus says:

> *Strive to enter through the narrow door. For many, I tell you, will*
> *seek to enter and will not be able. (Luke 13:24 NAS)*

Now, if you truly do find God, keep this in mind. If you find yourself falling away, ask yourself this question: Where am I going to go? We know that the only place to be is with God, under His power and His protection. Jesus likens our salvation to a tree.

> *I am the true vine, and My Father is the vine-dresser. Every branch*
> *in Me that does not bear fruit, He takes away; and every branch*
> *that bears fruit, He prunes it so that it may bear more fruit. You*
> *are already clean because of the word which I have spoken to you.*
> *Abide in Me, and I in you. As the branch cannot bear fruit of itself*
> *unless it abides in the vine, so neither can you unless you abide*
> *in Me. I am the vine, you are the branches; he who abides in Me*
> *and I in him, he bears much fruit, for apart from Me you can do*
> *nothing. If anyone does not abide in Me, he is thrown away as a*
> *branch and dries up; and they gather them, and cast them into the*
> *fire and they are burned. If you abide in Me, and My words abide*
> *in you, ask whatever you wish, and it will be done for you. My*
> *Father is glorified by this, that you bear much fruit, and so prove to*

be My disciples. Just as the Father has loved Me, I have also loved you; abide in My love. If you keep My commandments, you will abide in My love; just as I have kept My Father's commandments and abide in His love. These things I have spoken to you so that My joy may be in you, and that your joy may be made full. (John 15:1-11 NAS)

Notice that Jesus tells us to prove to be His disciple, and also that we abide in His love when we keep His commandments. This scripture clearly shows salvation as being a process we are continually experiencing. So how do we grow up in this relationship with God? The answer is by being obedient to Christ's word. In Matthew, Jesus gives us detailed instructions on how we should behave. *The outcome of our obedience is that we become God's children.*

But I say to you, do not resist an evil person: but whoever slaps you on your right cheek, give him the other also. And if any man will take away your tunic, let him have your cloak also. And whoever shall compel you to go a mile, go with him two. Give to him that asks you, and from him that would borrow of you turn not you away. You have heard that it has been said; you shall love your neighbor, and hate your enemy. But I say to you, Love your enemies, bless them that curse you, do good to them that hate you, and pray for them which spitefully use you, and persecute you; That you may be sons of your Father which is in heaven. (Matthew 5:38-45 KJV)

THE RIGHTEOUSNESS
OF GOD

But now a righteousness from God, apart from law, has been made known, to which the Law and the Prophets testify. (Romans 3:21 NIV)

Here, Paul speaks of a righteousness apart from the law. This righteousness is something that has to embody us. In other words we have to become this righteousness. This righteousness is from God and comes through faith in Jesus Christ.

The righteousness of God through faith in Jesus Christ for all who believe. (Romans 3:22 ESV)

The resurrection of Jesus Christ allows for believers to be endowed with the Spirit of Christ. This is how God becomes our righteousness. However, in this process, we become righteous. The Old Testament testifies of Christ becoming our righteousness:

Behold, the days are coming," says the Lord," That I will raise to David a Branch of righteousness; A King shall reign and prosper, and execute justice and righteousness in the earth. In His days

Judah will be saved, and Israel will dwell safely; Now this is His name by which He will be called.

THE LORD OUR RIGHTEOUSNESS. (Jeremiah 23:5)

This is accomplished by the grace of God. This is the righteousness of grace, righteousness that comes through faith so it is by the grace of God.

> *Therefore it is of faith, that it may be according to grace; to the end that the promise may be sure to all the seed; not to that only which is of the law, but to that also which is of the faith of Abraham, who is the father of us all. (Romans 4:16 KJV)*

This relationship with God is possible because Jesus went to the cross and provided reconciliation so we could have this relationship with God. Some people may be confused into thinking that grace does not require us to become righteous, because they believe that by faith alone we are saved. That may be true, but faith in Christ without righteousness will not allow us to enter the kingdom of God. Jesus died on the cross so that we could become righteous.

> *That the righteousness of the law may be fulfilled in us, who do not walk according to the flesh, but according to the Spirit. (Romans 8:4 KJV)*

As stated above, we should fulfill the righteousness of the law. If we want to be true disciples of Christ, we must live righteously by living the righteousness of faith.

But what does the righteousness of faith say? The word is near you;
it is in your mouth and in your heart, that is, the word of faith we
are proclaiming. (Romans 10:8 NIV)

How do we live the righteousness of faith? By being obedient to Jesus's word. Jesus says that if we truly follow His word, we will be set free from sin.

So Jesus was saying to those Jews who had believed Him, "If you
continue in My word, then you are truly disciples of Mine; And
you will know the truth, and the truth will set you free. (John
8:31-32 NASB)

Jesus is saying if you abide in His word, you will no longer continue to sin. Paul tells us in Romans that we should feel as though we have died and Christ now lives in us, because we were baptized into his death. As we give up our will, Christ can begin to live through us. This is how we are set free from sin. Jesus and Paul are saying the same thing here, only in different ways.

Or don't you know that all of us who were baptized into Christ
Jesus were baptized into his death? (Romans 6:3 NIV)

The word continues to repeat the same message. We have to become righteous. However, this righteousness comes not from us, but from God.

But now that you have been set free from sin and have become
slaves to God, the benefit you reap leads to holiness, and the result
is eternal life. (Romans 6:22 NIV)

FULFILLING THE WORD

The Gospel—the good news—is that God has put forth His word into our world, and that if we live His word, then we will be blessed.

> He replied, "Blessed rather are those who hear the word of God and obey it." (Luke 11:28 NIV)

This is a mystery of the gospel. Jesus fulfilled the word of God. Jesus's complete life was to fulfill those things that were written about him in the Old Testament. John the Baptist was also fulfilling the Old Testament. Both Jesus and John confirm this.

> The scroll of Isaiah the prophet was handed to him. He unrolled the scroll and found the place where this was written: "The Spirit of the Lord is upon me, for he has anointed me to bring Good News to the poor. He has sent me to proclaim that captives will be released, that the blind will see, that the oppressed will be set free, and that the time of the Lord's favor has come. He rolled up the scroll, handed it back to the attendant, and sat down. All eyes in the synagogue looked at him intently. Then he began to speak to them. "The Scripture you've just heard has been fulfilled this very day!" (Luke 4:17-21 NLT)

When John was asked who He was, He answered with a word from the Old Testament, saying he was the person spoken of there:

> John replied in the words of Isaiah the prophet, "I am the voice
> of one calling in the desert, 'Make straight the way for the Lord.'"
> (John 1:23 NIV)

In order to be part of the kingdom of God, we also must fulfill the word of God. Living the word of God becomes the righteousness of faith for us. Jesus says that the word He speaks is Spirit:

> It is the Spirit who gives life; the flesh is no help at all. The words
> that I have spoken to you are spirit and life. (6:63 NIV)

The words of Christ are Spirit and life. If we want to have the Spirit in us, we need to live the word that gives us life. We can also receive the Spirit when it is God's will, which gives us greater revelation from God. When we live the word, we fulfill the word and we witness to the word. Thus we help to bring the kingdom of God to earth.

> But you should keep a clear mind in every situation. Don't be
> afraid of suffering for the Lord. Work at telling others the Good
> News, and fulfill the ministry God has given you. (2 Timothy
> 4:5 NLT)

Paul speaks of the mystery of fulfilling the word:

> Of which I became a minister, according to the dispensation of
> God which is given to me for you, to fulfill the word of God, Even

the mystery which has been hid from ages and from generations,
but now is made manifest to his saints. (Colossians 1:25 ESV)

When Jesus was tempted by the devil, He showed us the way to overcome the devil: living by the WORD OF GOD.

Man shall not live by bread alone, but *every word that proceeds*
from the mouth of God. (Matthew 4:4 KJV)

PART C

The Kingdom of God Is Here

The Lord God will give him the throne of his father David, and he will reign over the house of Jacob forever; his kingdom will never end. (Luke 1:32-33 KJV)

JESUS STARTS THE KINGDOM

In the following pages, with the word of God, I will make the claim that the kingdom of God is here on earth, that it has been here for over 2000 years, and that it will continue forever, until the end of the world.

> And in the days of these kings shall the God of heaven set up a kingdom, which shall never be destroyed: and the kingdom shall not be left to other people, but it shall break in pieces and consume all these kingdoms, and it shall stand for ever. (Daniel 2:44 KJV)

This kingdom Daniel speaks of was created in the time of the Romans by God, through Jesus's ministry. Jesus said the kingdom of God is here.

> The time is fulfilled, and the kingdom of God is at hand; repent and believe in the gospel. (Mark 1:15 ESV)

Jesus says the time has come; God's kingdom is beginning. Repent, turn from your sin, and believe in the good news. The good news, or gospel, is that the kingdom of God has come: God has begun His rule on the earth. Jesus Christ started the kingdom. He gives us the teachings of the kingdom so that each disciple can follow God's teachings and do his part to bring forth the kingdom of God on earth. The Bible tells us that Jesus went through Galilee preaching the gospel of the kingdom.

> *Now Jesus went about all Galilee, teaching in their synagogues, preaching the gospel of the kingdom, and healing all kinds of sickness and all kinds of disease among the people. (Matthew 4:23 KJV)*

Some people want us to believe the gospel is that Jesus went to the cross to pardon our sins. However, the Bible tells us that Jesus was preaching the gospel while He was alive, as shown in the scripture above. When He sent the disciples to preach, He told them to preach, "Repent, the kingdom of heaven is at hand." The good news is that God has brought the knowledge of salvation to man, and in doing so has brought His reign. Christ is our King and Lord. His followers should be doing the will of God. We can only do this by Christ's redemption and by having His Spirit in us. When Jesus overcame death through the cross and resurrection from the dead, He was made King by God to rule His people forever. God says:

> *I have installed my King on Zion, my holy hill. (Psalm 2:6 NIV)*

The kingdom actually existed before Jesus came; the Jewish nation had the role of building the kingdom of God. God has always wanted this relationship, of being King over His people. But the Jewish nation wanted a human king to rule over them, like all the other nations of the world had. Here they ask for a king, not understanding that God was already their king:

> *No, but a king shall reign over us. When the Lord your God was your King.(1 Samuel 12:12 KJV)*

The Jewish nation had been the keeper of the kingdom, but as a nation they were not able to accomplish what God wanted them to do. They had lots of opportunities to listen to God.

> *Jerusalem, Jerusalem, who kills the prophets and stones those who are sent to her! How often I wanted to gather your children together, the way a hen gathers her chicks under her wings, and you were unwilling. (Matthew 23:37)*

After many years and many servants, God sends them His son in His final attempt to save the Jewish nation.

> *Finally he sent his son to them, saying, 'They will respect my son.' But when the tenants saw the son, they said to themselves, 'This is the heir. Come, let us kill him and have his inheritance. (Matthew 21:37, 38 ESV)*

After Jesus accomplished what he did on the cross, the kingdom was taken away from the Jewish nation and was given to Jesus Christ. Jesus would rule through the nation that would do God's will, through every believer who would do God's will.

> *Jesus said to them, Did you never read in the scriptures, The stone which the builders have rejected, has become the chief corner stone: this is the Lord's doing, and it is marvelous in our eyes? Therefore say I unto you, The kingdom of God shall be taken from you, and given to a nation bringing forth the fruits thereof. And whosoever shall fall on this stone shall be broken: but on whomsoever it shall fall, it will grind him to powder. (Matthew 21:42-43)*

The nation that holds the privilege of the kingdom must bring forth the fruits of the kingdom, which are righteousness, justice, mercy, faith, compassion for each other, defending the oppressed, helping the needy, and upholding law and order. Jesus clearly said the kingdom of God had arrived.

> But if I am casting out demons by the Spirit of God, then the Kingdom of God has arrived among you. (Matthew 12:28)

We see here in the book of Luke that Jesus will rule as a king. We just have to realize that Jesus is ruling on earth now and has been for over 2000 years.

> The Lord God will give him the throne of his father David, and he will reign over the house of Jacob forever; his kingdom will never end. (Luke 1:32-33 KJV)

Let's look more into this idea of the kingdom of God being on earth. If you want to be in the kingdom of God, you would do well to understand the kingdom of God.

UNDERSTANDING
THE KINGDOM

Let's look at one principle idea in the writings about Jesus. Jesus was accused of being a king; Pilate put this accusation on the cross. We could conclude that this is why the Romans agreed to crucify Him.

> And Pilate posted a sign on the cross that read, "Jesus of Nazareth, the King of the Jews." (John 19:19 NLT)

The Jewish leaders confirmed this accusation against Jesus, but protested the wording.

> Then the leading priests objected and said to Pilate, "Change it from 'The King of the Jews' to 'He said, I am King of the Jews.'"
> (John 19:21)

Did Jesus claim to be a king? Yes, He did, and rightly so, for He is King of Kings and Lord of Lords. The claim to be the messiah was also the claim to be a king, because the messiah would sit on the throne of David. The messiah would be the son of David.

> *He will reign on David's throne and over his kingdom, establishing*
> *and upholding it with justice and righteousness from that time on*
> *and forever. (Isaiah 9:7 NIV)*

Jesus purposely put into action this event to fulfill the prophecy shown below, saying that He was this king:

> *Jesus sent two disciples, saying to them, "Go to the village ahead of*
> *you, and at once you will find a donkey tied there, with her colt by*
> *her. Untie them and bring them to me. If anyone says anything to you,*
> *tell him that the Lord needs them, and he will send them right away."*
> *This took place to fulfill what was spoken through the prophet: "Say to*
> *the Daughter of Zion, 'See, your king comes to you, gentle and riding*
> *on a donkey, on a colt, the foal of a donkey.'" (Matthew 21:1-5 NIV)*

If you should find yourself rejecting what is being said here, it may be because you need the Spirit of God in order to understand it. Jesus said there were things we couldn't understand unless we were born again. If you want to know God's truth, pray that God may permit you to understand His truth and do what is needed to be born again. (See: Becoming Born Again)

> *Jesus replied, "I tell you the truth, unless you are born again, you*
> *cannot see (perceive) the Kingdom of God." (John 3:3 NLT)*

Paul also spoke about things that can't be understood unless you have the Spirit:

> *And I, brethren, could not speak to you as to spiritual men, but as*
> *to men of flesh, as to infants in Christ. (1 Corinthians 3:1 NAS)*

The Bible also tells us that scriptures have a veil over them and that Jesus is the one who can remove the veil.

> Then he *opened their minds*, that they might understand the Scriptures. (Luke 24:45 WEB)

Below, we see the mysteries of the kingdom that only God can allow us to understand:

> *He said, "The knowledge of the secrets of the kingdom of God has been given to you, but to others I speak in parables, so that, 'though seeing, they may not see; though hearing, they may not understand.'" (Luke 8:10 NIV)*

If you want to know God's truth, pray to God to be able to understand it, and He will answer.

> *For everyone who asks receives; he who seeks finds; and to him who knocks, the door will be opened. (Matthew 7:8 NIV)*

The followers of Christ were finding it hard to understand him. They had hopes that He was the promised Messiah. When Jesus was crucified, their hopes had been crushed. However, when Jesus rose from the dead, they had a renewed hope for His rule. In this scripture below, after Jesus rose from the dead, they asked Him a question.

> *So when they met together, they asked him, "Lord, are you at this time going to restore the kingdom to Israel?" (Acts 1:6)*

Jesus answered, saying it was not for them to know the time, but that they would receive power. What Christ was telling them is that they would receive power and they would be the ones to restore the kingdom. However, at that time they did not realize the enormity of what Jesus was saying.

> He said to them: "It is not for you to know the times or dates the
> Father has set by His own authority. But you will receive power
> when the Holy Spirit comes on you; and you will be my witnesses
> in Jerusalem, and in all Judea and Samaria, and to the ends of the
> earth. (Acts1:7-8)

We have the benefit of looking back through history. When we enter Saint Peter's church or a local church in our neighborhood, we know someone has witnessed for Christ and done his or her part in bringing the kingdom of God to earth, being His Witness, and giving glory to Jesus and to God. Understand and believe the scriptures, for Jesus Christ's kingdom has come. Ask yourself this question: Has Christ entered His glory? I say He has. Is there a greater glory possible beyond this glory? Yes: in the new heaven and the new earth which is to come. As our earth stands now and remains as such until the end of the this world comes, just as Jesus brought forth the kingdom of God we must continue in Gods work to bring the kingdom of God to earth.

> He said to them, "How foolish you are, and how slow of heart to
> believe all that the prophets have spoken! Did not the Christ have
> to suffer these things **and then** enter his glory? (Luke 24:25-26)

When you become born again, we have the right to become a subject of the kingdom of God, a servant of the King, of God, and of Christ.

Thus says the LORD, the King of Israel and his Redeemer, the LORD of hosts: "I am the first and I am the last; besides me there is no God. (Isaiah 44:6 ESV)

Here, we see God and Christ speaking in one voice, saying, 'I am the King and I am God.' If we are obeying God and he is our King, and He rules over our lives, then we are part of the kingdom and the kingdom of God has come to earth.

For he has rescued us from the kingdom of darkness and transferred us into the Kingdom of his dear Son. (Colossians 1:13 KJV)

If He doesn't rule over your life, then who does? This is what we need ask ourselves. Christ does not make us do what He wants. His followers do what He wants because we want to follow Him. We want to be like Him because we know that this is best for us.

It is enough for the disciple that he become like his teacher, and the slave like his master. (10:25 KJV)

What is the witness, then? It is that Christ died on the cross to reconcile us to God. Once we are reconciled to God, we can have a relationship with Him. Through this relationship and by God indwelling us with His Spirit, we should strive to overcome sin. The Kingdom of God is here on earth by the power God released into the world through the cross of Christ. Jesus has been appointed King in this kingdom and we must serve the King or reap the consequences of serving someone or something else.

WHO ENTERS
THE KINGDOM

Those who fulfill the word of God are the ones who go to the kingdom of heaven, because they are the ones who bring the kingdom of God to earth. This is done with the reconciliation that the cross of Christ gives us, and with the power given to us by God. Jesus says you must be greater than John the Baptist to enter the kingdom of Heaven. In other words, we must do more than John did.

> *Verily I say unto you, among them that are born of women there has not arisen a greater than John the Baptist: yet he that is least in the kingdom of heaven is greater than he. (Matthew 11:11 KJV)*

Why is John least? Because he was the forerunner, he announced the savior. John is the beginning of the gospel; as the beginning, he is least. John prepared the way for the Lord.

> *The beginning of the gospel about Jesus Christ, the Son of God. It is written in Isaiah the prophet: "I will send my messenger ahead of you, who will prepare your way"—"a voice of one calling in the desert, 'Prepare the way for the Lord, make straight paths for him.'" (Mark 1:1-3 NIV)*

Jesus then reveals the truth of God and accomplishes the reconciliation of man with God. Jesus brought forth the power of God into this world, and John announced it. Now Jesus's followers, armed with this knowledge and power, must continue God's work. Jesus said we would do more than He did.

> I tell you the truth, anyone who has faith in me will do what I have been doing. He will do even greater things than these, because I am going to the Father. (John 14:12 KJV)

We would do more than Jesus because we will have more time than He did, God willing. Jesus went to the cross at the age of thirty-three, and most people now live longer than that. We have more time to do God's will. In order to go to the kingdom of heaven, we must bring people into the kingdom of God on earth. Those who hear the word of God: understand it, do it, and teach that others will go to heaven.

> But the one who received the seed that fell on good soil is the man who hears the word and understands it. He produces a crop, yielding a hundred, sixty or thirty times what was sown. (Matthew 13:23 NIV)

Those who do the will of God on earth are the ones who go to the kingdom of Heaven.

> Not everyone who says to me, 'Lord, Lord,' will enter the kingdom of heaven, but the one who does the will of my Father who is in heaven. On that day many will say to me, 'Lord, Lord, did we not prophesy in your name, and cast out demons in your name, and do many mighty works in your name?' And then will I declare to them,

'I never knew you; depart from me, you workers of lawlessness.'
(Matthew 7:21-23 ESV)

We should always try to be the people God wants us to be. Salvation is a daily relationship with God.

> *Strive to enter through the narrow gate, for many I tell you will*
> *seek to enter but will not be able. (Luke 13:24 ESV)*

Peter confirms that salvation is to be sought after. Salvation is to be sought out, lived out, and taught to others.

> *Therefore, brethren, be more diligent to make your calling and*
> *election sure, for doing these things ye will never fall; for so an*
> *entrance will be supplied to you abundantly into the everlasting*
> *kingdom of our Lord and Savior Jesus Christ. (2 Peter 1:10-11)*

As Jesus says in a previous scripture, those who do God's will go to heaven. The will of God is that we obey His word, and in doing so, we are sanctified by it. This should be our witness to others. If you have another witness, the Lord says to take heed to your witness. For it is written:

> *For this is the will of God, your sanctification; that is, that you*
> *abstain from sexual immorality; that each of you know how to*
> *possess his own vessel in sanctification and honor, not in lustful*
> *passion, like the Gentiles who do not know God; and that no*
> *man transgress and defraud his brother in the matter because the*
> *Lord is the avenger in all these things, just as we also told you*
> *before and solemnly warned you. For God has not called us for the*

purpose of impurity, but in sanctification. So, he who rejects this is not rejecting man but the God who gives His Holy Spirit to you. (1 Thessalonians 4:1 NASB)

To defraud someone in this matter is to tell someone they are saved without telling them that they need to overcome sin and how to do it. Search the scriptures and you will see this is true. Are you a companion in the kingdom of God, as John states here?

I John, who also am your brother, and companion in tribulation, and in the kingdom and patience of Jesus Christ, was in the isle that is called Patmos, for the word of God, and for the testimony of Jesus Christ. (Revelation 1:9 KJV)

Do you have the testimony of Jesus Christ? John was imprisoned for testimony of the word of God and of Jesus Christ. There is only one testimony. Jesus is the Savior, the son of God and the King of this world. You have to serve Him if you want to be part of His kingdom.

FOUNDATIONS
OF THE KINGDOM

Jesus is the cornerstone and the foundation of the kingdom of God.

> *For no one can lay any foundation other than the one already laid,*
> *which is Jesus Christ. (1 Corinthians 3:11 NIV)*

Jesus's teachings are the building blocks of the kingdom of God, because Jesus received these teachings directly from God.

> *Do you not believe that I am in the Father and the Father is in me?*
> *The words that I say to you I do not speak on my own authority, but*
> *the Father who dwells in me does his works. (John 14:10 ESV)*

God has throughout time tried to teach mankind how they should live. Jesus was given the greatest revelation of how man should live. No one has a greater revelation of God than Jesus Christ.

> *It is written in the Prophets, 'And they will all be taught by God.'*
> *Everyone who has heard and learned from the Father comes to me.*
> *(John 6:45 ESV)*

We must implement these teachings into our lives and our children's lives if we want to achieve the life that God has in store for us. It is not enough to know the word; we must live the word. The word has to be part of who we are.

> But what does it say? *"THE WORD IS NEAR YOU, IN YOUR MOUTH AND IN YOUR HEART"*—that is, the word of faith which we are preaching. (Romans 10:8 NAS)

Righteousness is the power of Christ's Kingdom, and it is given to us by God.

> This is the heritage of the servants of the LORD, and their righteousness is of me, said the LORD. (Isaiah 54:17 KJV)

We must attain righteousness by having the Holy Spirit. We must preach righteousness to be part of the kingdom of God.

> Your throne, O God, is forever and ever; A scepter of uprightness is the scepter of Your kingdom. have loved righteousness and hated wickedness; Therefore God, Your God, has anointed You With the oil of joy above Your fellows. (Psalm 45:6-7)

On the foundation of Christ's teachings and with the righteousness granted to us through the Holy Spirit, we must build a structure of unity between the churches of Christ. We must be united in Christ. This is God's will; that all Christians should love one another. Regardless of our disagreements, we should strive to get along with each other. If we want to be builders of His kingdom and not destroyers of it, then we must be united.

> *Every kingdom divided against itself will be ruined, and every*
> *city or household divided against itself will not stand. (Matthew*
> *12:25 KJV)*

All Christians, from every denomination in Christ, should get along with one another. Everyone who confesses that Jesus is the Christ, the word of God, reveals this truth.

> *Everyone who believes that Jesus is the Christ has become a child*
> *of God. And everyone who loves the Father loves his children, too.*
> *(1 John 5:1 KJV)*

The denominations of Christianity need to unite under this common foundation.

Even though there are some serious differences of opinion about doctrine, Jesus still requires us to get along as Christians. This is how we know if we are following Jesus Christ.

> *By this all men will know that you are my disciples, if you love one*
> *another. (John 13:35 KJV)*

If as Christians we don't have love for one another, then can we really call ourselves Christians? If you don't follow Jesus's teachings, then you are not really a Christian, even if you think you are. This may sound harsh, but we should all examine ourselves to see if we are really on God's side.

> *He who is not with me is against me, and he who does not gather*
> *with me scatters. (Matthew 12:30 NIV)*

Are you gathering people for God and telling them to follow Jesus Christ, and to become like Christ? Each one of us that becomes like Christ has also become one more stone in the building that forms the kingdom of God on earth.

> *Do not be afraid, little flock, for your Father has been pleased to give you the kingdom. (Luke 12:32 NIV)*

PROPHECIES
OF THE KINGDOM

There are many scriptures that prophesy about the kingdom of God. However, one that stands out from all of them is from the book of Daniel:

> *In the time of those kings, the God of heaven will set up a kingdom*
> *that will never be destroyed, nor will it be left to another people.*
> *It will crush all those kingdoms and bring them to an end, but it*
> *will itself endure forever. This is the meaning of the vision of the*
> *rock cut out of a mountain, but not by human hands—a rock that*
> *broke the iron, the bronze, the clay, the silver and the gold to pieces.*
> *(Daniel 2:44 NIV)*

In this scripture, Daniel is interpreting a dream for King Nebuchadnezzar. Daniel tells of a statue that represents a succession of kingdoms. Most scholars agree that these kingdoms are Babylon, the Persian Empire, the Grecian Empire, and the fourth kingdom being the Roman Empire. Daniel explains that during the time of the Romans that the God of heaven is going to start a kingdom that will last forever. Some believe that this will not happen until Jesus's second coming, but the scriptures tell a different story. Although it is not widely accepted, however it is the truth: Jesus began the kingdom spoken of here, in the book of Daniel. When Jesus went to the cross and fulfilled the will of the Father, God made Him King of the world. You may think that this is not true; how could God's kingdom be here, with all that is going wrong? However, this is the wrong question to ask. Think about how it would be if Jesus had never come and accomplished all He did. Also, think about the idea of every Christian trying to create the kingdom of God on earth by following and teaching Jesus's teachings, and giving all the glory to God. Man has not fulfilled what God prepared for him because he has not followed the truth. The lack of paradise on earth is not a failure on God's part; it is due to man's inability to fulfill Jesus Christ's teachings and to do God's will. In the book of Matthew Jesus makes reference to Daniel's prophecy. There are a lot of things that match up with this scripture mentioned here to the book of Daniel.

> *"The stone that the builders rejected has now become the cornerstone. This is the Lord's doing, and it is wonderful to see. I tell you, the Kingdom of God will be taken away from you and given to a nation that will produce the proper fruit. Anyone who stumbles over that stone will be broken to pieces, and it will crush anyone it falls on. (Matthew 21:42-43 NLT)*

In these scriptures, God is the one who sets up the kingdom. Jesus is the stone that is rejected, but He becomes the cornerstone that crushes all the kingdoms. These other kingdoms are gone, but not Christ's kingdom. His rule is continuing and going strong through the church. The churches of Jesus Christ are the kingdom of God on earth. If you still think Jesus is not ruling in this world, just think of how many people call Jesus 'Lord.' If Jesus is Lord with many servants, then He is ruling in this world. Let's look at more scripture about Jesus Christ's kingdom.

> *Of the increase of his government and peace there will be no end. He will reign on David's throne and over his kingdom, establishing and upholding it with justice and righteousness from that time on and forever. The zeal of the LORD Almighty will accomplish this. (Isaiah 9:7 NIV)*

Notice the similarity between this scripture and Luke's scripture below. Luke is telling us with almost the same words that Jesus is a fulfillment of the prophecy by Isaiah.

> *He will be great and will be called the Son of the Most High. The Lord God will give him the throne of his father David, and he will reign over the house of Jacob forever; his kingdom will never end. (Luke 1:32-33 NIV)*

We must ask ourselves: has this already happened? The answer is yes. Jesus has become very great. He reigns over all His people and His rule has already lasted for over 2000 years. The churches of Jesus have to learn that they are instructed by Jesus Himself to teach God's word, not what they think the gospel is. It is time for the churches of Jesus Christ to implement the rule of God by teaching men to follow Jesus Christ's teachings, as was His command.

> *Therefore go and make disciples of all nations, baptizing them in the name of the Father and of the Son and of the Holy Spirit, and teaching them to obey everything I have commanded you. And*

surely I am with you always, to the very end of the age. (Matthew 28:19-20 NIV)

Jeremiah speaks of a king who will reign on the earth. Are you part of this branch?

"Behold, the days are coming," says the Lord," That I will raise to David a Branch of righteousness; A King shall reign and prosper, and execute justice and righteousness in the earth. In His days Judah will be saved, and Israel will dwell safely." (Jeremiah 23:5)

We know that Jesus was a descendant of David. Jesus witnessed that He was the true vine or branch. He also witnessed that He was a king. By the power of God as the servants of God, we should, as Christians, execute justice and righteousness on the earth and be the light of the world, as Jesus told us we should be.

You are the light of the world. A city on a hill cannot be hidden. Neither do people light a lamp and put it under a bowl. Instead they put it on its stand, and it gives light to everyone in the house. In the same way, let your light shine before men, that they may see your good deeds and praise your Father in heaven. (Matthew 5:14-1616 NIV)

Jesus Christ reigns as King of this world through every believer who believes and lives according to the word of God. These believers will execute justice and righteousness in the world. This is the kingdom of God, and Jesus started it over 2000 years ago. This is very important for us as believers, because if the kingdom has come and we don't know or understand it, then how can we serve God in His kingdom? How can we do God's will?

> *The Lord is gracious and merciful; slow to anger and abounding in steadfast love. The Lord is good to all, and his mercy is over all that he has made. All your works shall give thanks to you, O Lord, and all your saints shall bless you! They shall speak of the glory of your kingdom and tell of your power, to make known to the children of man your mighty deeds, and the glorious splendor of your kingdom. Your kingdom is an everlasting kingdom, and your dominion endures throughout all generations. (Psalm 145:8-13 ESV)*

PART D

The Blessed Life

Blessed are those who hunger and thirst for righteousness, for they will be filled. (Matthew 5:6 KJV)

THOSE WHO BELONG
ARE BLESSED

Those who are transferred into the kingdom are blessed. We are transferred into the kingdom when we are ruled by God and no longer ruled by Satan.

> *To open their eyes and turn them from darkness to light, and from the power of Satan to God, so that they may receive forgiveness of sins and a place among those who are sanctified by faith in me. (Acts 26:18 NIV)*

As it says in the scripture above, we must have forgiveness of our sins, and sanctification, and then we are part of the kingdom.

> *Always thanking the Father. He has enabled you to share in the inheritance that belongs to his people, who live in the light. For he has rescued us from the kingdom of darkness and transferred us into the Kingdom of his dear Son. (Colossians 1:13-14 NLT)*

The kingdom is every person who acknowledges Jesus Christ as King and serves Him. If we truly do become Christ's followers, we receive blessings for being obedient to His word. Those who belong to the kingdom are blessed.

> *Blessed is the kingdom of our father David that is coming in the name of the Lord! Hosanna in the highest! (Mark 11:10)*

If we can grasp this idea that we are God's workmanship, then we are in a state of mind in which we can ask, 'God, what will you make of me today?'

> *For we are God's workmanship, created in Christ Jesus to do good works, which God prepared in advance for us to do. (Ephesians 2:10 KJV)*

This is how God's kingdom comes to earth: by His followers doing the will of God, and asking, 'God, what do you want me to do?' If God doesn't speak to you directly, then follow Jesus's teachings the Bible. If you live according to His words, you will be building your house on the rock.

> *Everyone then who hears these words of mine and does them will be like a wise man who built his house on the rock. And the rain fell, and the floods came, and the winds blew and beat on that house, but it did not fall, because it had been founded on the rock. And everyone who hears these words of mine and does not do them will be like a foolish man who built his house on the sand. And the rain fell, and the floods came, and the winds blew and beat against that house, and it fell, and great was the fall of it. (Matthew 7:24-27 ESV)*

HOW TO BE BLESSED

If we follow Christ's teachings, then we will be blessed.

> *Now that I, your Lord and Teacher, have washed your feet, you*
> *also should wash one another's feet. I have set you an example that*
> *you should do as I have done for you. I tell you the truth, no servant*
> *is greater than his master, nor is a messenger greater than the one*
> *who sent him. Now that you know these things, you will be blessed*
> *if you do them. (John 13:14-17)*

We will be blessed if we meditate on the word of God.

> *Blessed is the man that walks not in the counsel of the ungodly,*
> *nor stands in the way of sinners, nor sits in the seat of the scornful.*
> *But his delight is in the law of the LORD; and in his law does*
> *he meditate day and night. And he shall be like a tree planted*
> *by the rivers of water, that brings forth his fruit in his season; his*
> *leaf also shall not wither; and whatever he does shall prosper. The*
> *ungodly are not so: but are like the chaff which the wind drives*
> *away. Therefore the ungodly shall not stand in the judgment, nor*
> *sinners in the congregation of the righteous. For the LORD knows*

the way of the righteous: but the way of the ungodly shall perish.
(Psalm 1:1-6 KJV)

Blessings belong to those who give.

That he himself said, 'It is more blessed to give than to receive.'
(Acts 20:35)

God will reward those who do deeds to please Him.

But when you give to the needy, do not let your left hand know
what your right hand is doing, so that your giving may be in
secret. And your Father who sees in secret will reward you.
(Matthew 6:3-4)

Blessings abound if you become who the Lord wants you to become.
Live the word.

Blessed are the poor in spirit, for theirs is the kingdom of heaven.
Blessed are those who mourn, for they will be comforted. Blessed
are the meek, for they will inherit the earth. Blessed are those who
hunger and thirst for righteousness, for they will be filled. Blessed
are the merciful, for they will be shown mercy. Blessed are the pure
in heart, for they will see God. Blessed are the peacemakers, for
they will be called sons of God. Blessed are those who are persecuted
because of righteousness, for theirs is the kingdom of heaven.
(Matthew 5:3-10)

These are not financial blessings; they are blessings that surpass material
wealth. These are blessings for our flesh.

My children, pay attention to what I say. Listen carefully to my words. Don't lose sight of them. Let them penetrate deep into your heart, for they bring life to those who find them, and healing to their whole body. (Proverbs 4:20-22)

YOUR ACCOUNT IN HEAVEN

This section is about how we are rewarded for our obedience to God. We must begin with the understanding that we are judged according to our deeds, even as believers in Christ. Both the Old and New Testaments have many scriptures that confirm this. Paul confirms it in the book of Romans:

> *Who WILL RENDER TO EACH PERSON ACCORDING TO HIS DEEDS: to those who by perseverance in doing good seek for glory and honor and immortality, eternal life; but to those who are selfishly ambitious and do not obey the truth, but obey unrighteousness, wrath and indignation. There will be tribulation and distress for every soul of man who does evil, of the Jew first and also of the Greek, but glory and honor and peace to everyone who does good, to the Jew first and also to the Greek. For there is no partiality with God. (Romans 2:6-11 NASB)*

We see the same witness in the Old Testament:

> *Don't excuse yourself by saying, "Look, we didn't know." For God understands all hearts, and he sees you. He who guards your soul*

knows you knew. He will repay all people as their actions deserve.
(Proverbs 24:12 NLT)

God says specifically to the church that he will reward us according to
our works.

And all the churches will know that I am he who searches mind
and heart, and I will give to each of you according to your works.
(Revelation 2:23 KJV)

As believers in Jesus, we should be trying to do God's will. As you do
deeds, God determines your worthiness; God then credits your account
in Heaven, which results in your place in the kingdom that is on earth
and your eternal destination. This is about your relationship with God,
and how we serve our God, the King.

Do not be afraid, little flock, for your Father has been pleased to
give you the kingdom. Sell your possessions and give to the poor.
Provide purses for yourselves that will not wear out, a treasure in
heaven that will not be exhausted, where no thief comes near and
no moth destroys. For where your treasure is, there your heart will
be also. (Luke 12:32-34)

What do you treasure? Riches, material belongings, or perhaps
something else? Do you treasure your relationship with God? If your
treasure is with God, so will your actions be.

Do not lay up for yourselves treasures on earth, where moth and
rust destroy and where thieves break in and steal, but lay up for
yourselves treasures in heaven, where neither moth nor rust destroys

and where thieves do not break in and steal. For where your treasure is, there your heart will be also. (Matthew 6:19-21 ESV)

God is seeking a relationship with us in which we do what He says and He rewards us accordingly:

So that your giving may be in secret. Then your Father, who sees what is done in secret, will reward you. (Matthew 6:4 KJV)

This shows Him that we love Him.

If you love me, you will obey my commandments. (John 14:15 GWT)

We see in this scripture that those who overcome sin are rewarded. Throughout this book, it has been shown that it is sin we must overcome. (See: Living Without Sin)

He, who has an ear, let him hear what the Spirit says to the churches. To him who overcomes, I will give the right to eat from the tree of life, which is in the paradise of God. (Revelation 2:7 KJV)

Look very closely at this scripture. Those who don't overcome sin are erased from the book of life:

He who overcomes will thus be clothed in white garments; and I will not erase his name from the book of life, and I will confess his name before My Father and before His angels. (Revelation 3:5 NASB)

Our place in the kingdom of God on earth is dependent on our account in heaven. Is it not time for us to shine as the light of the world, as Christ requires of us? REMEMBER, IF WE DON'T, GOD WILL FIND FOLLOWERS WHO WILL.

CONCLUSION

In conclusion, God has put forth a sacrifice for us that we might be reconciled to Him: Jesus Christ, our Lord. God gave us this atonement so we could become righteous people living for Him, by receiving God's spirit and by living His word.

Once reconciled, we begin our relationship with God. Jesus's life is a model for us to follow so that we may be obedient to God's will. When God is ready, He will supply us with power through His holy Spirit. While we wait for God to bless us with His Spirit, we have His word to keep us in touch with Him, because His word is Spirit as well.

Our salvation is the completion of all that God does through us while we are here on earth, and our eternity is a representation of our lives. A righteous life will result in reward, and an evil life will result in condemnation. God started His rule on earth over 2000 years ago, and it will continue on until Jesus returns and destroys this world with the glory of His appearance. Then He will create the new heaven and the new earth.

But the day of the Lord will come like a thief, in which the heavens
will pass away with a roar and the elements will be destroyed with

intense heat, and the earth and its works will be burned up. Since all these things are to be destroyed in this way, what sort of people ought you to be in holy conduct and godliness, looking for and hastening the coming of the day of God, because of which the heavens will be destroyed by burning, and the elements will melt with intense heat! But according to His promise we are looking for new heavens and a new earth, in which righteousness dwells. (2 Peter 3:10-13 NASB)

Until then, God wants this message proclaimed to the whole world: Jesus Christ is the King of the world. Being our Lord and King we must obey Him in order to be in His kingdom.

> *I have installed my own king on Zion, my holy mountain. (Psalm 2:6 GWT)*

As for me, I am whatever the Lord makes me.

Ron
A disciple of Christ

Visit our website for more information: www.totheelect.com

PART E

Doctrines of Christianity

Take heed to yourself, and to the doctrine; continue in them: for in doing this you shall both save yourself, and them that hear you. (1 Timothy 4:16 KJV)

In this section, I will cover some specific doctrinal issues in order to give clarification on specific terms not covered in detail in their own sections.

THE ATONEMENT

Jesus's death on the cross is an atonement for our sins. We are all under the rule of sin; this sin separates us from God.

> For all have sinned and fall short of the glory of God. (Romans 3:23 NIV)

God sent Jesus to atone for our sin so that we could be reconciled to God. When we believe and accept this sacrifice God gave for us, we are reconciled to God.

> For if, when we were God's enemies, we were reconciled to him through the death of his Son, how much more, having been reconciled, shall we be saved through his life! (Romans 5:10 NIV)

Notice in this scripture we are reconciled to God "through the death of His Son," but this is not the entirety of our salvation. Paul continues with "how much more will we be saved through His life in us." Christ's life should be our life; His spirit dwells in us, which is also our life. Our salvation is both the atonement (our reconciliation) and who we become, now that we are the children of God.

Therefore, if anyone is in Christ, he is a new creation; the old has gone, the new has come! All this is from God, who reconciled us to himself through Christ and gave us the ministry of reconciliation: that God was reconciling the world to himself in Christ, not counting men's sins against them. And he has committed to us the message of reconciliation. We are therefore Christ's ambassadors, as though God were making his appeal through us. We implore you on Christ's behalf: Be reconciled to God. God made him who had no sin to be sin for us, so that in him we might become the righteousness of God. (2 Corinthians 5:17-21)

In this scripture, we see that anyone who is in Christ is a new creation, just as we were born in the flesh and have to grow up. When we are born again, we also have to grow up in our spiritual birth. This new birth is from God, and by God, it is all His grace. We are not meant to convict, but to show people the way. Jesus is our reconciliation, *so that we might become the righteousness of God.* Understand that we have to become the righteousness of God.

> *This is the heritage of the servants of the LORD, and their righteousness is of me, said the LORD. (Isaiah 54:17 NIV)*

Because Christ's death and the atonement God supplied for us have reconciled us to God, God wants us to know that we must learn His righteousness.

> *Though grace is shown to the wicked, they do not learn righteousness; even in a land of uprightness they go on doing evil and regard not the majesty of the LORD. (Isaiah 26:10 NIV)*

You see, if we regard His majesty, then we obey His word. Jesus died on the cross so that we might be reconciled to God. His death is an atonement for our sins. Once reconciled to God, we must become the people God wants us to be. Jesus died on the cross to remove sin from our world.

Behold the lamb of God who takes away the sin of the world. (John 1:29 ESV)

FAITH

You have probably heard someone say something like this or you might have said it yourself: 'You don't know there is a God; you just have to believe, that is what faith is all about.' In fact, that is not what faith is. Faith is *what we believe*, not just 'believing.' You might ask what the difference is. There is a big difference. Why? When it comes to the matter of our salvation, *what we believe makes all the difference*. If you believe a lie, then you will not find the truth. That is why what we believe makes all the difference. For example, let's look at this very popular scripture:

> *For by grace you have been saved through faith; and that not of yourselves, it is the gift of God; not as a result of works, so that no one may boast. (Ephesians 2:8-9 NAS)*

By grace, we are saved through faith. Does that mean we are saved by believing? Or are we saved by *what we believe*? This is a very popular scripture. Problems arise from it when people think that they are saved because they believe. What we have to understand is that we are saved by *what we believe*, and *when we use what we believe, we now have to bring in all the teachings of Jesus, everything He said*. Don't believe me; believe the word. What did Jesus tell us to do?

Therefore, go and make disciples of all the nations, baptizing them in the name of the Father and the Son and the Holy Spirit. Teach these new disciples to obey all the commands I have given you. And be sure of this: I am with you always, even to the end of the age.

We know that salvation is to be hoped for. The scripture below tells us that faith should generate confidence in what we hope for. Also, faith actually gives us evidence that God exists. In other words: Faith, *what we believe*, shows us evidence of God. Therefore, what we believe is crucial to whether we find God or not.

Now faith is the substance of things hoped for, the evidence of things not seen. (Hebrews 11:1 KJV)

Faith is the realization of things hoped for. Faith will produce evidence of what we believe. How does faith show the existence of God? If you believe what the word says and then apply it, God will show you evidence of His existence. For example, the scripture says:

When you give to the needy, do not announce it with trumpets, as the hypocrites do in the synagogues and on the streets, to be honored by men. I tell you the truth, they have received their reward in full. But when you give to the needy, do not let your left hand know what your right hand is doing, so that your giving may be in secret. Then your Father, who sees what is done in secret, will reward you. (Matthew 6:2-4 NIV)

The key is that you must live your faith in order to experience it. When you experience the reward from God, then you will know God is real.

Elect of God, we know that you have faith. However, know this: faith without faithfulness to God is no faith at all.

> *The Lord rewards every man for his righteousness and faithfulness.*
> (1 Samuel 26:23 NIV)

JUSTIFICATION

The doctrine of justification, one of many doctrines of Christianity, plays a major role in understanding Christianity. The most important issue in considering justification is whether the word tells us that being justified actually accomplishes our complete salvation. Or, does justification reconcile us to God and begin our salvation? It may seem like there is no big difference between these two. However, the distinction is the difference between knowing the truth and not knowing it. It is a problem if you believe that justification is salvation, for then the power of God is blocked. If you read the book of Romans with the idea that justification accomplishes reconciliation, you will see, God willing, that justification brings reconciliation, which is the beginning of our salvation, not the completion of it.

> *Since we have now been justified by his blood, how much more shall we be saved from God's wrath through him! For if, when we were God's enemies, we were reconciled to him through the death of his Son, how much more, having been reconciled, shall we be saved through his life! (Romans 5:9-10 NIV)*

In these scriptures, we can clearly see that there are two parts to our salvation. We are justified by His blood and saved through His life.

Justification is reconciliation; salvation is being saved from our sin by removing sin out of our lives by having His Spirit live in us. If justification was complete salvation, then Paul couldn't say the things he says about not sinning.

> *What shall we say then? Are we to continue in sin that grace may abound? By no means! How can we who died to sin still live in it? (Romans 6:1-2 ESV)*

If justification was complete salvation, why would Paul say we should fulfill the law?

> *Well then, if we emphasize faith, does this mean that we can forget about the law? Of course not! In fact, only when we have faith do we truly fulfill the law. (Romans 3:31 NLT)*

We also see in the book of Romans that being led by the Spirit is essential for salvation.

> *If you are living according to the flesh, you must die; but if by the Spirit you are putting to death the deeds of the body, you will live. For all who are being led by the Spirit of God, these are sons of God. (Romans 8:13-14 NASB)*

The key to justification is that once we enter that place where we are considered righteous before God, we must become righteous by the spirit of God in order to stay there.

Do you not know that if you present yourselves to anyone as obedient slaves, you are slaves of the one whom you obey, either of sin, which leads to death, or of obedience, which leads to righteousness? (Romans 6:16 ESV)

May the Lord be with you, Amen.